CW00550764

SOSR
Dismissals

By Daniel Barnett

The Employment Law Library

All books in the Employment Law Library are sent for free to members of the HR Inner Circle.

1. Employee Investigations
2. GDPR for HR Professionals
3. Preventing and Defending Employee Stress Claims
4. Employment Tribunal Time Limits
5. Deconstructing TUPE
6. Changing Terms & Conditions
7. Constructive Dismissal
8. Resolving Grievances
9. HR Hazards
10. Employment Status
11. Spotting Malingering
12. Employment Tribunal Compensation
13. Hiring Staff
14. Computer and Social Media Misuse
15. Managing Sickness Absence
16. The Three Ps
17. Conflict at Work
18. SOSR Dismissals
19. Dismissing Problem Employees

Published by Employment Law Services Limited, Unit 3, Chequers Farm, Chequers Lane, Watford, Hertfordshire WD25 0LG

Whilst the publishers and the authors have taken every care in preparing the material included in this work, any statements made as to the legal or other implications of particular transactions are made in good faith purely for general guidance and cannot be regarded as a substitute for professional advice. Any liability is limited to the purchase value of this book or £100, whichever is the greater.

© Employment Law Services Ltd 2024. All rights reserved.

ISBN 978-1-913925-16-1

EMPLOYMENT
LAW
MATTERS

Subscribe to
Daniel Barnett's podcast
EMPLOYMENT LAW MATTERS
via iTunes, Spotify, or your
favourite podcast player

WWW.DANIELBARNETT.CO.UK/PODCAST

 iTunes  Spotify

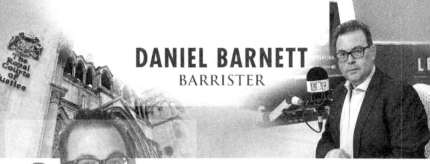

DANIEL BARNETT
BARRISTER

SUBSCRIBE

HOME   PLAYLISTS   COMMUNITY   CHANNELS   ABOUT

Try these

CAN PRESIDENT TRUMP PARDON HIMSELF?
6:57

HELP I'M BEING BULLIED AT WORK
13:45

LBC
7:05

HOW TO HANDLE DISCIPLINARY DISMISSAL AND PERFORMANCE MANAGEMENT SITUA...
1:53:34

Trump

Help - I'm being bullied at work: a practical guide for...
Daniel Barnett
4.5K views • 3 weeks ago

The most heartbreaking, emotional call I've ever take...
Daniel Barnett
1.2K views • 3 weeks ago

How to Handle Disciplinary, Dismissal and Performance...
Daniel Barnett
688 views • 1 month ago

ASK THE PRESIDENT
EMPLOYMENT TRIBUNALS PRESIDENT (E&W) JUDGE BARRY CLARKE
1:13:52

FAIRNESS IN REDUNDANCY SELECTION
REBECCA TUCK QC
44:01

HELP I'M BEING BULLIED AT WORK
13:45

Ask the President: Judge Barry Clarke, President of ...
Daniel Barnett
views • 2 weeks ago

Fair Redundancy Dismissals with Rebecca Tuck QC
Daniel Barnett
1K views • 2 weeks ago

Help - I'm being bullied at work: a practical guide for...
Daniel Barnett
4.5K views • 3 weeks ago

LAW

THE UK'S LEADING
YOUTUBE CHANNEL FOR
LAW EXPLAINER VIDEOS

BIT.LY/YOUTUBELEGAL

About the Author

 Daniel Barnett is a leading employment law barrister practising from Outer Temple Chambers. With 30 years' experience defending public and private sector employers against employment claims, he has represented a Royal Family, several international airlines, FTSE-100 companies and various NHS Trusts and local authorities. Employee clients include David & Victoria Beckham's nanny and Paul Mason (subject of the ITV documentary 'Britain's Fattest Man').

Daniel is a past chair of the Employment Lawyers' Association's publishing committee and electronic services working party. He is the author or co-author of eight books, including the Law Society Handbook on Employment Law (currently in its 9th edition). He is the creator of the Employment Law (UK) mailing list, an email alerter bulletin service sending details of breaking news in employment law three times a week to 33,000 recipients.

Legal directories describe him as 'extremely knowledgeable and [he] can absorb pages of instructions at lightning speed', 'involved in a number of highly contentious matters', 'singled out for his work for large blue-chip companies', 'combination of in-depth legal knowledge, pragmatism, quick response times and approachability', 'inexhaustible', 'tenacious', 'knowledgeable', and 'an excellent advocate'.

He is one of the leading speakers and trainers on the employment law and HR circuit. He has presented seminars for the House of Commons, the BBC, Oxford University, HSBC, Barclays Bank, Ocado, and dozens of other organisations in-house. In 2013, 2014, 2016, and 2019 he designed — and was the sole speaker at — the Employment Law MasterClass national tour.

As well as full-time practice as a barrister and speaker, Daniel is the founder of the HR Inner Circle – a membership club for smart, ambitious HR Professionals. In 2007, he co-founded CPD Webinars Ltd, then the UK's leading webinar training company for lawyers, and sold it to Thomson Reuters in 2011.

Daniel is widely sought after as a commentator in both broadcast and print media on all legal issues. Since 2010 he has presented the Legal Hour on LBC Radio. In 2019, he launched Employment Law

Matters, a weekly podcast with short explanations of employment law topics. Subscribe at www.danielbarnett.co.uk/podcast

www.danielbarnett.co.uk

Temple, London

The new edition of this invaluable handbook provides a
comprehensively updated overview of employment law.
Fully revised and rewritten, it covers:
Employment status
Unfair and wrongful dismissal
Discrimination
Redundancy
Transfer of undertakings
Health & safety at work
Remedies and compensation
Tribunal procedure
Written by experts in the field, this book is authoritative,
clear and reader friendly.
Visit
WWW.EMPLOYMENTLAWHANDBOOK.COM
for more information.

Acknowledgments

This is book 18 in the series of mini-guides on employment law for HR professionals. None of these books are possible without the input and experience of the members of the HR Inner Circle. I write these small books for you, and you get them for free as part of your membership. Many of the ideas in this book were drawn from members' experiences and questions in our online community and on our Q&A calls.

I'd like to thank Becky Ranauta for her help with the content of this book.

Thanks also to Susan Keillor and Josh Powell for their comments on the draft manuscript, Tincuta Collett for the layout and design, Aaron Gaff for proofreading and Maria Rodriguez for converting the book into the formats needed for Amazon.

If you're not a member of the HR Inner Circle and you're interested in learning more about HR Inner Circle membership (www.hrinnercircle.co.uk), there is some information at the back of this book.

Daniel Barnett
March 2024

Table of Contents

Introduction

There are all sorts of reasons why you might perfectly reasonably want to dismiss an employee, but doing so without a fair reason can easily backfire.

All employees with two or more years' service are protected from unfair dismissal, and those with less service can pursue a raft of alternative claims, so establishing a genuine 'fair reason' is vital.

And it's this that can make 'some other substantial reason' – better known as 'SOSR' – an option worth exploring. There are not many restrictions on what can potentially amount to a SOSR dismissal, but there's also a catch: whatever it is, the reason has to be genuine. You can't just dress something up as SOSR when you should have taken a different route to dismissal or, indeed, play the SOSR card where there is no proper SOSR reason at all.

For example, if the actual reason for dismissal is somebody's behaviour leading to a breakdown in relationships, that would normally be categorised as a 'conduct' dismissal. You can't explain away, for example, non-compliance with the *Acas Code of Practice on Disciplinary and Grievance Procedures* (Acas Code) by saying, "Oh, but it's SOSR" and hoping the tribunal will allow you to get away with ignoring the Acas Code.

'SOSR Dismissals' is a meticulously crafted guide that empowers HR professionals and employers with the knowledge and tools to manage SOSR dismissals effectively. It's an essential resource for anyone seeking to navigate the complex landscape of employment law with confidence, ensuring both legal compliance and fairness in the challenging but vital task of workforce management.

To begin, it is important to establish a foundational understanding of what constitutes SOSR within the framework of employment law. This book articulates the necessity for HR professionals to distinguish SOSR from other dismissal reasons, such as conduct or capability issues, thereby setting the tone for a detailed and informative journey through this aspect of employment law.

Each chapter of the book delves into specific elements and applications of SOSR.

Chapter 1 provides a thorough definition of SOSR, discussing its place under the *Employment Rights Act 1996* and its flexibility compared to other dismissal reasons. This chapter sets the stage for understanding how SOSR can be a viable option in situations where traditional dismissal reasons may not apply.

In Chapter 2, the focus shifts to what makes a SOSR dismissal fair. This chapter is particularly valuable as it addresses the critical importance of identifying the real reason for dismissal – a misstep in this regard can lead to significant legal challenges. Through practical examples, the chapter illustrates how mislabelling the reason for dismissal can lead employers down the wrong procedural path, potentially resulting in unfair dismissal claims.

Chapter 3, dedicated to outlining a fair SOSR procedure, is a practical guide for HR professionals. It emphasises that while SOSR provides flexibility, it still demands a fair and reasonable process. This chapter is particularly insightful, providing a step-by-step guide to ensure procedural fairness and compliance with legal standards.

Chapters 4 to 9 explore various scenarios in which SOSR can be applied, such as business reorganisations, the expiration of fixed-term contracts and dismissals arising from TUPE situations. These chapters are rich with real-life examples and case studies, offering readers a practical understanding of how SOSR is applied in different contexts. The book discusses how

SOSR can be a practical solution in situations like personality clashes and third-party pressures, or when an employee's conduct outside of work poses a risk to the employer's reputation.

The book is not only about understanding when and how to use SOSR but also about mastering the nuances of executing it correctly. For instance, it discusses how to handle situations where the Acas Code might apply to SOSR dismissals. This is crucial, as failure to comply with the Acas Code can lead to increased compensation awards in tribunal cases.

Throughout, the book acknowledges the grey areas and complexities inherent in SOSR dismissals and offers pragmatic advice for navigating these. For HR professionals, this means not just understanding the law but also knowing how to apply it in a way that balances legal compliance with the realities of managing a workforce.

Chapter 10 provides a succinct yet comprehensive summary. It reiterates the key points from each chapter, offering a quick refresher on the main themes and takeaways. This summary is an invaluable tool for HR professionals to review key concepts and reinforce their understanding.

This book summarises the law in England, Wales and Scotland. It does not apply to Northern Ireland or countries outside the UK.

CHAPTER 1
What defines SOSR?

Employees with more than two years' service are protected from unfair dismissal under the *Employment Rights Act 1996*. To be a 'fair' dismissal, the reason must be one of the following:

- Listed under section 98(2) of the *Employment Rights Act 1996* as a potentially fair reason. There are four reasons listed: (i) conduct; (ii) capability or qualifications; (iii) redundancy; and (iv) illegality.

- For 'some other substantial reason of a kind such as to justify the dismissal of an employee holding the position which the employee held'.

This book is about the latter.

SOSR enables a fair dismissal to take place even when the reason (or principal reason) for dismissal is not one of the four listed in section 98(2) of the *Employment Rights Act 1996*. There are few restrictions on what might count as SOSR; it need not be based on anything particularly sophisticated or complex. In fact, the only statutory definition is that set out in the *Employment Rights Act 1996*, quoted above. There is no further guidance in the *Employment Rights Act 1996*, which is where unfair dismissal law is located.

There is therefore flexibility in what might be a fair SOSR, and many different scenarios potentially qualify. Examples, all of which are addressed in this book, include business reorganisations, personality clashes, refusal to accept changes to terms and conditions or expiry of a fixed-term contract.

Although there are benefits to this flexibility, it can also make SOSR difficult to get to grips with as there is no clear employer checklist. That said, the courts and tribunals have over the years developed different categories of SOSR that provide some clarity and structure.

What is clear is that a made-up reason will not work – even if it sounds plausible. To succeed, the reason should be based on a stance a reasonable employer would adopt, and it also needs to be sufficiently 'substantial'. SOSR is not a cure-all panacea – anything that appears frivolous or insignificant to an employment tribunal won't be regarded as a fair reason.

CHAPTER 2

What makes a SOSR dismissal fair?

A tribunal will want to work out the real reason for dismissal. The label the employer has put on it is of little value if the tribunal disagrees.

For example, two employees who don't get on can end up damaging a team dynamic. This could be due to the bad behaviour of one (or both) of the employees, or just a personality clash with neither being at fault. Whilst the employer is trying to resolve matters, the underlying reason – whether performance, conduct or personality clash – won't matter a huge amount as the focus will be on finding a solution to the problem.

However, once it comes to dismissing one (or both) of the employees, the reason will become much more important. To get this right, the question to ask is, "What is the real reason we want to dismiss the employee?" If it is their bad behaviour, then the correct fair reason is 'conduct', and the disciplinary procedure will need to be completed before dismissal. If it is a no-fault personality clash, SOSR will likely be more appropriate and there will be more flexibility in the manner of dismissal.

The risk of mislabelling the reason for dismissal is that you follow the wrong dismissal process. Although tribunals may sometimes give an employer the benefit of the doubt where there's an innocent mistake (and it is reasonable for the employer to have made that mistake), they will take a dim view if the mislabelling is deliberate, for example, to avoid complying with the Acas Code or giving warnings before dismissal. So, if the real reason for dismissing an employee is that you can no longer tolerate their persistent non-compliance with rules and their sub-standard attitude, but to avoid following a disciplinary procedure you pretend it is due to a blameless personality clash, the tribunal is likely to spot this ploy and swiftly deliver a finding of unfair dismissal.

The employee's seniority within the business can also influence the outcome. In *Cobley v Forward Technology Industries plc*, for example, the Court of Appeal said that the chief executive officer's dismissal following a successful company takeover was a fair dismissal for SOSR. However, with more junior staff, SOSR would not have been a fair reason as the takeover did not affect their employment relationship in the same way.

That said, whatever the reason for dismissal, what is more important is that the employer has been fair – and that's where the real challenge lies. This flowchart offers basic guidance on whether or not to follow the SOSR route.

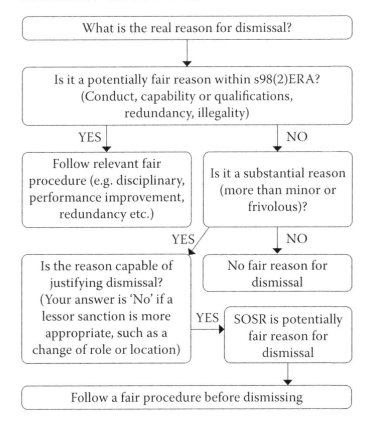

A fair reason in itself is not enough to make a dismissal fair. It is a two-part process, and the employer must show that:

1. SOSR is the reason, or the main reason, for the dismissal.

2. The decision to dismiss for SOSR was reasonable in all the circumstances (section 98(4) of the *Employment Relations Act 1996*). This is the usual test of what is fair, taking into account the size of the business, the resources available to it, the merits of the case and the procedure followed.

As usual with the law on unfair dismissal, it is this second part of the test where the majority of traps lie for unsuspecting employers. But it can be even more tricky when dealing with SOSR because of the variety in the type of dismissal it can cover.

This means there is no established one-size-fits-all route to arriving at a fair dismissal. Contrast this with, for example, the fair reasons for 'conduct' or 'capability', where an employer has to follow its disciplinary, performance improvement or absence procedures to secure a fair dismissal.

For SOSR, what is fair will always depend on the particular circumstances.

Does the Acas Code apply?

Like everything else to do with SOSR, the answer to this question is fluid. In other words, whether the Acas Code applies depends on the circumstances.

But it's important to get this right. Getting it wrong is expensive. Failure to comply with the Acas Code (when it does apply) will likely mean the overall process is unfair and will also lead to an increase (or 'uplift') in the employee's award by up to 25%.

The Acas Code states:

'This Code is designed to help employers, employees and their representatives deal with disciplinary and grievance situations in the workplace.

- Disciplinary situations include misconduct and/or poor performance. If employers have a separate capability procedure, they may prefer to address performance issues under this procedure. If so, however, the basic principles of fairness set out in this Code should still be followed, albeit that they may need to be adapted.

- Grievances are concerns, problems or complaints that employees raise with their employers. The Code does not apply to redundancy dismissals or the non-renewal of fixed-term contracts on their expiry.'

As a reminder, the Acas Code says employers should:

- Establish the facts of each case (by investigation).

- Inform the employee of the problem and invite them to a meeting.

- Allow the employee to be accompanied at the meeting.

- Decide on appropriate action.

- Inform the employee of the decision.

- Give the employee the opportunity to appeal.

So the Acas Code neither expressly applies to SOSR dismissals nor excludes them (as it excludes redundancy dismissals) and the expiry of fixed-term contracts. This has left the courts to step in and try to clear up some of the confusion.

Lund v St Edmunds School, Canterbury

The employee, Mr Lund, became frustrated with his employer's computer equipment and systems. This led to him destroying the equipment, behaving erratically and being difficult and unhelpful towards other staff. The employer dismissed him and relied on SOSR as the potentially fair reason on the basis of a breakdown in their relationship.

The tribunal found that the dismissal was unfair. However, it said the Acas Code did not apply because the reason for dismissal was SOSR, not conduct, and did not make any uplift to the employee's award. The Employment Appeal Tribunal (EAT) disagreed and said the Code *did* apply. The reference in the Acas Code to 'disciplinary situations' should be construed broadly, and it will apply where:

- Disciplinary proceedings were (or ought to have been) invoked against the employee.
- The outcome of those proceedings might have led to disciplinary action against the employee.

In this case, it was the employee's conduct that lay behind the dismissal, and there was undoubtedly a 'disciplinary situation'. Therefore, the Acas Code applied.

Phoenix House v Stockman

The employee, Ms Stockman, alleged that she had been mistreated by the finance director. She raised a grievance against him and confronted him in front of another member of staff. Following grievance and disciplinary proceedings (while the employee was on sick leave), the employer attempted to repair the relationship via mediation. However, this was unsuccessful and, following a formal meeting with the employee, she was dismissed for SOSR, based on the alleged breakdown of the working relationship. This was despite the employee saying in the meeting that she was prepared to return to work and to continue to work with the finance director.

The tribunal upheld the employee's unfair dismissal claim for several reasons, including the employer's failure to comply with the Acas Code. The EAT agreed that the employee had been unfairly dismissed but said that the Acas Code did not apply because:

- There is no clear wording in the Acas Code saying it applies to SOSR dismissals.

- There was no 'disciplinary situation' in this case, as neither misconduct nor capability was alleged.

- In these circumstances, it would be unfair to punish the employer (by increasing the compensation awarded) given it had not been forewarned of the risk.

However, the EAT said that where parts of the Acas Code are capable of being applied in a SOSR situation, they should be. In this case, the EAT considered that before being dismissed, the employee should have been given the opportunity to show that she could fit back into the workplace without undue disruption.

The Acas Code is therefore likely to apply in full if there is a 'disciplinary situation' where the employer thinks the employee is guilty of misconduct or sub-standard performance. If that's the case, then it is best to comply with the Acas Code. However, do be honest: although it may be tempting to turn a blind eye to the employee's culpability and instead use SOSR for dismissal, a tribunal will not be easily fooled. The true motive for dismissal will likely be uncovered and the tribunal will then come down hard on an employer that has attempted to mislead it.

Even if there is not a 'disciplinary situation', the EAT's decision in *Phoenix House* suggests employers should always keep the Acas Code in mind when dismissing for SOSR. In this case, the employer's failure to give the employee the opportunity to show that she could fit back into the workplace meant it had not 'decided on appropriate action' in a fair manner. The EAT described this as 'ordinary common-sense fairness' and using this yardstick, it is easy to see how the Acas Code's principles could be applied to all sorts of other SOSR dismissals too.

Therefore, it's well worth applying any parts of the Acas Code that seem relevant to the situation. Not only will this act as an insurance policy against the cost of an uplift but it will also help build the secure foundations of a fair dismissal.

CHAPTER 3

A fair SOSR procedure

Regardless of the application of the Acas Code, a fair SOSR dismissal will generally involve some sort of fair procedure. What this means in practice can vary depending on the precise reason for dismissal, but as a minimum, it should generally include:

- Carrying out some form of investigation, even if only to decide how best to proceed, for example, whether to deal with the issues under a disciplinary procedure or to take another path.

- Warning, discussing, and consulting with the employee about the issues before deciding to dismiss. Usually, this will include one or more meetings at which the employer should explain the circumstances that may lead to dismissal and give the employee the chance to respond.

- Giving the employee the opportunity to appeal.

Also, for the decision to dismiss to be reasonable in all the circumstances, it will usually be necessary to consider alternatives to dismissal. These normally include moving the employee to another team, role or location.

Whether the dismissal is fair will be judged at the time employment terminates, not the date that the initial decision to dismiss was taken. This means that employers should be prepared to switch tack if circumstances change. For example, suppose an employer needs to make changes to terms and conditions but the employee objects. Here, the employer may dismiss the employee on notice for SOSR with the intention of offering re-engagement on the new terms. If, however, the disgruntled employee starts going AWOL during their notice period and takes unauthorised time off work, the employer may decide not to offer re-engagement. In this case, the employer should change tack and follow a disciplinary procedure because the real reason for dismissal will more likely be misconduct.

Ultimately, the fairness of a SOSR dismissal will be judged on the process as a whole. This is helpful as it then becomes less of a tick-box exercise and can give employers more freedom. Unlike a misconduct dismissal, there is not always the need to pre-warn the employee of the reasons for a potential dismissal in such clear terms. In *L v K*, the Court of Session found the dismissal for SOSR (risk to the employer's reputation) to be fair, despite this reason not being set out in the letter to the employee inviting him to the dismissal meeting. The Court said it was enough that the possibility of dismissal for this reason was discussed at that meeting. But it's still better to be clear about the proposed reason for dismissal in a letter: you just have a greater chance of defeating an unfair dismissal claim if your process falls below expected practice. As some say, if it's not documented, it didn't happen!

The flexibility in a SOSR dismissal can extend (very occasionally) to allowing an employer to avoid following any sort of dismissal procedure altogether. Here are three examples in which the courts considered the impact of a poor, or absent, dismissal process.

Gallacher v Abellio Scotrail Limited

In this case, the relationship between two senior managers became strained because of various disputes, including salary disputes. This impacted poorly on the employer, and the company started to trade at a loss. The employer decided it needed to make changes quickly. As there were no signs the relationship could be repaired and no alternative roles available, the employer dismissed the more junior employee without any disciplinary procedure or offer of appeal.

The EAT said this was a fair dismissal, despite the lack of process, as there would have been nothing useful to be gained by doing otherwise and, in fact, this may have made the situation worse.

Hawkes v Ausin Group

Here, the employee made clear he was determined to attend a (voluntary) seven-week training course despite it taking place during a very busy period for the employer. The employer was small, still in its first year of trading, and the employee was the most senior member of staff. For these reasons, the employee's absence would be seriously detrimental to its financial health, so it called a meeting at which it dismissed the employee with immediate effect and payment in lieu of notice.

The EAT agreed that this was a fair dismissal given the size and circumstances of the employer and that an earlier meeting or warnings would have been pointless.

Moore v Phoenix Product Development

In this case, the EAT found the dismissal by the employer of its founder and ex-CEO was fair, despite the lack of appeal. Any further meetings (including an appeal) would have been pointless given the employer's small size (with no higher level of management) and the extent of the 'irreparable' breakdown in the relationship, which had been caused by the employee's behaviour.

However, it is very important to note that the circumstances illustrated in these cases will be rare. Most of the time, employers will need to follow some form of process or face the (expensive) consequences.

CHAPTER 4

When can you (confidently) use SOSR?

Any number of reasons could ultimately amount to SOSR. However, as a result of court and tribunal decisions on SOSR, certain categories have taken shape over time and include the following.

- **Business reorganisation:** Where jobs are reorganised into different, new roles – and there is a genuine and substantial business reason for the change – any resulting dismissals can be for SOSR. However, this should only be used where there is no reduction in the need for a particular number of employees. If there *is* a reduction in need for the number of employees, the reason for dismissal would be redundancy (which, of course, is one of the established 'fair' reasons for dismissal).

- **Changing terms and conditions:** Employers need to change contractual terms and conditions for multiple reasons, such as altered working patterns, a new location and pay. Where an employee refuses to accept the change, this can result in their dismissal for SOSR. However, the employer must be able to show that the changes are necessary and for sound business reasons. See Book 6 in the Employment Law Library on Changing Terms and Conditions.

- **Personality clash:** Where personality clashes are causing substantial disruption to the business and the employer has taken all reasonable steps to try to resolve the issue, any subsequent dismissal can be for SOSR. See Book 17 in the Employment Law Library on Conflict at Work.

- **Client (or other third party) pressure:** External pressure, for example from a client or supplier, can amount to SOSR. However, whether it will succeed depends on a number of factors, including weighing up the third party's business value (and the impact if it was lost) against the injustice to the employee if they were dismissed.

- **Risk to reputation:** This can amount to SOSR when the risk to reputation is genuinely and sufficiently serious, for example, where an employee has been accused of a criminal offence and the employer is concerned about the effect on its reputation of continuing to employ them.

- **Conflict of interest:** Commercial conflicts of interest can arise where, for example, an employee has a close relationship with someone who works for a competitor. If this gives rise to a real commercial risk, then this can amount to a fair SOSR.

- **Dismissal for an ETO in the context of a TUPE transfer:** The *Transfer of Undertakings (Protection of Employment) Regulations 2006* say that dismissal connected to the transfer of an employee's employment from one employer to another will be potentially fair for SOSR if there is an economic, technical or organisational (ETO) reason. See Book 5 of the Employment Law Library on Deconstructing TUPE.

- **Expiry of a fixed-term contract:** The dismissal of an employee due to the non-renewal of their fixed-term contract can be for SOSR. Whether such a dismissal is fair will depend on the (genuine) reasons for non-renewal and how far in advance the end date was made clear to the employee.

- **Temporary employees:** Where an employee is recruited to provide temporary cover for an absent member of staff, their dismissal upon the absentee's return to work will automatically be potentially fair for SOSR (section 106 of the *Employment Rights Act 1996*). This applies to medical or maternity absence, pregnancy or childbirth, adoption or shared parental leave. However, to rely on this, the employer should inform the temporary employee, in writing (at the time they are recruited), that their employment will terminate when the other employee returns to work. The employer should also consider whether there is any suitable alternative employment for the temporary employee before dismissal.

- **Mistake or ignorance of the law:** Where an employer dismisses an employee due to a genuine but mistaken belief about the law, this can be fair for SOSR. However, the employer will need a good reason for making the mistake, for example, genuinely believing immigration law would be breached by continuing to employ an individual or mistakenly interpreting an employee's hint that they intended to leave the business as an actual resignation.

- **Breakdown in trust and confidence:**
  Where an employee is dismissed because the employer reasonably believes it no longer has any trust and confidence in the employee, the dismissal can be fair for SOSR. But if the lack of trust and confidence flows from misconduct or poor performance, then *that* (i.e. misconduct or capability) should be relied on as the reason for dismissal, not SOSR. In other words, trust and confidence should not be used to avoid following the proper procedures required for another fair reason.

The next chapter explores these categories in more detail.

CHAPTER 5

Business reorganisation

One of the only certainties in business is change.

Fortunately, the law recognises this, and fundamentally, employers have the right to run their businesses as they like – including reorganising the structure.

When dismissing, one pitfall to avoid is mislabelling the reason for dismissal. Although SOSR can be the correct way to justify a dismissal resulting from a business reorganisation, if there is (or could be) a reduction in the number of roles or type of work, the real reason for dismissal is redundancy. In that case, you'll need to follow a redundancy procedure, including fair selection, individual (and collective) consultation, looking for alternative employment and paying redundancy payments.

If the number of roles remains stable, then SOSR may be a way of justifying dismissal where, for example, the existing work is blended into different, new roles, but the employee does not fit into the new structure.

However, establishing SOSR as a potentially fair reason is part of establishing a fair dismissal. Under section 98(4) of the *Employment Rights Act 1996*, the decision to dismiss for SOSR must also be reasonable in all the circumstances. This includes following a fair procedure.

Fair procedure

A fair procedure in the context of a business reorganisation is likely to include:

- Consultation about the proposed reorganisation (and any selection process if required)
- Warning of the risk of dismissal
- Looking for alternative employment
- Offering a right to appeal

In fact, it is likely to end up being broadly similar to a redundancy process, just without the need to make a statutory redundancy payment (although many employers will choose to make a redundancy payment anyway).

Changing terms and conditions

Even if the employee's role is still required within the new structure, they may refuse to accept it, most likely because of changes they're not keen on, such as different working patterns or pay.

If the changes are relatively minor – for example, tweaks to the job description – they may not amount to a contractual change and, even if they do, you might be entitled to vary them under the terms of the employment contract.

However, in most cases, contractual changes will be more fundamental, whether as part of a business reorganisation or just day-to-day management. For example, you may need to change an employee's shift pattern or remove a contractual right to overtime pay to save costs.

Sometimes, these changes can be made with the employee's agreement, particularly if you throw in a 'sweetener' (or two). However, where an employee refuses to accept such contractual changes, you are likely to need to rely on SOSR if you want to dismiss.

Sound, good business reason

You'll need a sound, good business reason for a change in terms and conditions, particularly if it leads to dismissal. Don't invent one, though: it needs to be genuine. It also needs to be objectively reasonable, so think about whether another (reasonable) employer might agree with you.

That said, your motive for imposing change does not need to be so significant that if you did not make the change the whole business would implode. There just needs to be a clear advantage to the business in doing so.

Even if your reason is good, make sure you can back it up with evidence. For example, in *Banerjee v City and East London*, the EAT said that an employee was unfairly dismissed when the employer made his role full-time after his job-share partner left. Despite the fact the employer had a policy of amalgamating part-time consultancies into full-time posts, it could produce no evidence of the advantages of the policy or the importance attached to it.

Fairness of dismissal

Try to be objective about this. Weigh up how reasonable it may seem for you to dismiss an employee who refuses to accept a change to their terms and conditions versus how reasonable the employee may be in refusing the change. Why? If you end up at an employment tribunal fighting an unfair dismissal claim, this is the balancing act the tribunal will carry out.

The tribunal can take a wide range of factors into account as part of this exercise. These might include the proportion of employees accepting or rejecting the change, or the effect of the change on them. Are they left considerably out of pocket?

However, none of these factors will be conclusive on their own. Ultimately, to decide where the balance lies, the full context needs to be taken into account.

For example, in *St John of God (Care Services) Ltd v Brooks*, a hospital faced with a severe cash crisis proposed to make changes to employees' terms and conditions that would reduce both their pay and holiday entitlement. Out of 170 employees, 140 accepted the new terms, and the 30 who refused were dismissed. The employment tribunal upheld their unfair dismissal claims. It said their refusal to accept the changes was reasonable in light of their severity and the hospital had acted unreasonably in dismissing them.

However, the EAT disagreed. It said that the impact of the changes on the employees was not determinative of fairness. The situation also needed to be viewed through the prism of the hospital's cash crisis, which cast a more positive light on the reasonableness of the employer's actions. It is feasible that an employee is reasonable in their refusal to accept changes, but that their dismissal is still fair.

So, in the right circumstances, even the most draconian changes to terms and conditions can result in a fair dismissal for SOSR. However, as usual, this will depend on following a fair procedure.

Fair procedure

A fair procedure will generally include:

- **Consultation:** Discussions with affected employees about the proposed changes need to be meaningful – that is, open-minded and two-way. Remember that if the changes may result in the dismissal and/or re-engagement of more than 20 employees at one establishment within a rolling 90-day period, you will also need to collectively consult.

- **Clear communication:** Explain the full effect of the changes and the business reasons behind them, and provide as much information as possible – preferably in writing. Also outline any potential (and worse!) alternatives, including dismissal if this is a realistic outcome, if the proposed changes are not implemented. However, be careful not to sound threatening.

- **Listening:** Listen to employees' concerns about the changes. Respond reasonably to objections and make concessions where possible.

- **Voluntary agreement:** Use your best persuasive techniques to sell the changes and get your employees' agreement.

- **Exploring alternatives:** Try to find an alternative solution to dismissal.

- **Offering to re-engage:** If affected employees really will not agree, rather than just imposing change on them, it is generally better to terminate their old contracts lawfully on notice and offer to immediately re-engage them on the new terms.

This last step (termination and re-engagement) has hit the headlines in recent years and has been given the pretty harsh-sounding label of 'fire and rehire'. Indeed, it's become rather a controversial topic, not helped by the number of employers who resorted to it during the Covid pandemic to try to counter falling profits. The public outcry against this practice got even louder following the dismissal by P&O Ferries of approximately 800 employees without notice by a pre-recorded Zoom meeting and their subsequent replacement by cheaper agency workers.

The upshot is that the government has produced a statutory code to try to tackle the perceived problems.

Statutory code of practice

The 'Code of Practice on Dismissal and Re-engagement' (the Code) is still in draft at the time of writing, but its main principles are unlikely to be revised. This is to provide best practice guidance (and a step-by-step process) for employers to follow when making changes to terms and conditions, with a view to avoiding dismissals.

Although the Code does not ban employers from dismissing employees due to their refusal to accept contractual changes, any (unreasonable) failure to comply with the Code can result in an uplift to an employee's unfair dismissal award of up to 25%. It is therefore worth paying attention to.

Importantly, the Code applies whenever an employer wants to make contractual changes and contemplates dismissing those employees who do not agree. This is regardless of whether the plan is to offer them re-engagement on new terms, or (like P&O) to replace them with new staff on new terms.

That said, the good news is that many of the recommended steps in the Code are already established by case law and are part of good employee relations practice. In that sense, it is unlikely that the Code will have much impact on the current requirements for a fair SOSR dismissal.

However, the Code does aim to slow the pace of change, so be careful to complete a fair SOSR procedure. In particular, the Code recommends that employers:

- Take their time to consult and give as much notice as possible of the changes
- Spread the introduction of multiple changes to terms and conditions over a period of time
- Resist using the threat of dismissal to pressure employees into quick agreement
- Actively re-examine – and be prepared to change – a business strategy if agreement cannot be reached (rather than dismiss)
- Keep changes under review and consider reintroducing the previous terms if the original reason for changing them ceases to be relevant
- Only dismiss as an absolute last resort.

If you want to learn more about this topic, see Book 6 of the Employment Law Library on Changing Terms and Conditions.

Personality clash

It would be great if the workplace was a guaranteed safe space where everyone got on well with each other at all times. Unfortunately, human nature does not generally work like that. There are bound to be people who just don't see eye to eye with each other, or with their employer.

Sometimes, the cracks in a personality clash can be smoothed over with a compromise, but you may occasionally need to consider dismissing one (or both) of the employees involved. SOSR can be a fair reason for such dismissals. Remember, the reason must be 'substantial' and capable of justifying dismissal. In other words, the personality clash must be so bad that it's causing substantial disruption to the business and that despite trying everything to resolve the issue, dismissal is your last resort.

This is a pretty high hurdle to clear, particularly for larger employers that tribunals perceive as having the resources to avoid such drastic action. However, if you're a smaller employer, your tolerance levels may well be lower (and the tribunals' higher).

For example, in *Treganowan v Robert Knee and Co Ltd*, a small employer's dismissal of an 'over-sharing' employee was found to be fair. Ms Treganowan told her two female colleagues that she had an illegitimate child and was sleeping with a man "almost half her age". The EAT judge held that the dispute was over the dispute of the extent of the "permissive society". Her recounting of these matters created an uncomfortable atmosphere at work, which seriously affected business. As a small employer, the options for dealing with the situation were limited and, having exhausted all angles for resolution, it was reasonable to dismiss. The case was decided in 1975; it is very much a creature of its age.

More recently, in *Gallacher v Abellio Scotrail Limited*, a personality clash between two senior employees (discussed in Chapter 3) had a substantial impact on a small employer's financial situation, and the more junior employee's dismissal was viewed by the tribunal as a proportionate response.

In *Phoenix House Ltd v Stockman* (discussed in Chapter 2), the EAT said that for an employer to dismiss fairly for SOSR, it is not enough that two employees are not getting on. The relationship has to be at the point of no return, with no reasonable prospect of the employees ever being able to work together again. This is a high test to meet.

Even if an impact is substantial, to amount to SOSR, the reason for dismissal needs to be based on something more than just the employee's personality. There needs to be a clash. For example, in *Perkins v St Georges Healthcare NHS Trust*, although the finance director's personality was tricky, it was his personal attacks on other senior colleagues that ultimately formed the fair reason for dismissal.

If the action stemming from the personality issue amounts to misconduct or poor performance, make sure you deal with this under the disciplinary or capability process instead.

Perhaps even more importantly, if the action could be an expression – or 'manifestation' – of an employee's protected belief under the *Equality Act 2010*, then take extra care with how you handle the situation, particularly as the courts have made clear that a wide spectrum of beliefs is worthy of protection and that only those that are most extreme – for example, Nazism – will fall outside it.

Labelling an employee with protected beliefs as 'difficult' is likely to open up a Pandora's box of criticism from both the tribunal and the wider public. So, if you dismiss, make sure you have very clear examples of how the employee's behaviour had a substantial (and negative) impact on the organisation. Otherwise, you'll likely end up fighting a claim not only for unfair dismissal but also for discrimination.

Fair procedure

If the personality clash is bad enough to establish SOSR as a potentially fair reason for dismissal, then you can move on to the next stage of making sure your decision to dismiss is reasonable. This includes following a fair procedure.

Remember, a fair SOSR procedure should generally include:

- Investigation (in this case into the causes of the conflict)
- Meeting(s) with the employee – to allow them to have their say
- Warning(s) that dismissal is a possible outcome
- The right to appeal

The following steps are also particularly relevant to a personality clash:

- Try to resolve the conflict – for example, through mediation, counselling or training. See the information box on mediation, below.
- Consider alternatives to dismissal, such as transferring the employee to a different department or team or changing reporting

lines or work patterns to avoid those involved coming into contact.

Only if the relationship is irreparable and the situation cannot continue will a SOSR dismissal likely be fair.

Some thoughts on Mediation

As Robert Burns so famously said, *"O wad some Power the giftie gie us. To see oursels as ithers see us!"*

Mediation can really help two conflicting parties appreciate, or at least get a better understanding of, each other's point of view. It's not about finding a compromise. Mediation is about understanding and resolution. Often, both sides tell exactly the same story. They hate the situation they've got themselves into and they believe the other person is either enjoying it or at least driving it. And when they hear the other person thinks exactly the same, it can be a revelation and can totally change their mindset.

Often, one employee will say, "I had no idea you thought X because I thought you thought Y," and the other will say, "How could you possibly think I thought Y, because Z?" And it all goes uphill from there.

As with most things going uphill, it needs a push. You need a good mediator. They vary in quality, but if you get a good one, it's like alchemy.

Antony Sendall, a mediator from a firm called mediationrescue.co.uk spoke at the HR Inner Circle Annual Conference in 2023, and everyone in the room had one of those 'this sounds better than I thought' lightbulb moments. If you're a member of the HR Inner Circle, you can find the talk in the members' area of the website.

When you raise mediation with your HR Director or COO, you might get pushback along the lines of "But mediation is expensive". What you've got to do is ask, "Expensive compared with what?" A £1,500-£3,000 fee to know the problem is probably going to get solved is a lot better than the cost of another six months of conflict before one of the two employees resigns and brings a constructive dismissal claim, followed by the cost and hassle of recruiting somebody else for the role and hoping they work out.

Mediation needs people to engage in brutally honest reflection about their own behaviour and the impact they have on other people. It can involve very powerful emotions –

including anger, remorse, regret and shame – and some mediations end up needing boxes of tissues. And it can work wonders.

Risk to reputation

Reputation matters, not only in the private sector where it has a direct impact on profits but also in the public sector where the glare of scrutiny can be blinding.

It is therefore good news that where an employee poses a risk to an employer's reputation, they can be fairly dismissed for SOSR.

However, to justify dismissal, the risk posed to the employer's reputation has to be really severe and have the potential to cause substantial harm to its business interests. Further, the employer needs clear evidence of the actual or likely risk were the employee to remain employed, and dismissal should only be relied on as a last resort.

Given this high threshold, it is unsurprising that the few cases where employers have relied on this as a SOSR reason tend to involve alleged criminal activity.

For example, in *Wadley v Eager Electrical Ltd*, a long-serving employee was dismissed for SOSR because his wife (who worked for the same company) was convicted of theft. Although the EAT said this could amount to SOSR, the lack of evidence connecting the wife's conduct to loss of customers meant that it was not.

However, in *Lafferty v Nuffield Health*, the employer did successfully rely on risk to reputation when it dismissed a long-serving hospital theatre porter with an exemplary record who was charged with, but not convicted of, assault with intent to rape. The EAT said the dismissal was fair as the employer was reasonable and genuine in its concern that continuing to employ the porter risked substantial harm to its reputation. The employee had access to vulnerable patients and the employer was a not-for-profit charity that was under particular public scrutiny at the time in light of recent scandals in the sector.

That said, as usual, the fairness of the dismissal will very much depend on the context and the reasonableness of the employer's actions – including following a fair procedure.

Fair procedure

As well as following the usual steps for a fair SOSR procedure (see 'Personality clash', above), additional tips for risk to reputation include the following:

- Focus your investigation on the risk to the organisation suffering damage to its reputation rather than on trying to determine whether the employee is guilty of the underlying offence.

- Where an employee has been accused of a criminal offence:

  * Ensure the investigation is well documented and that any action taken is not a knee-jerk reaction.

  * Take steps to find out as much as possible about the charges made. Take into account the seriousness with which the police (or other investigating body) are treating the allegations. If they prosecute, it is serious. However, remain objective and do not accept the evidence uncritically.

  * Only use a criminal charge as a ground for dismissal if there is a clear connection between the alleged offence and the employee's duties and responsibilities.

Conflict of interest

Employers are entitled to protect their commercial interests against threats posed by their employees' actions.

Most commonly, the root cause of the threat is the employee's misconduct. In that case, you need to follow your disciplinary procedure.

However, from time to time, a commercial conflict of interest can arise in which the employee is not (obviously) to blame – for example, where an employee has a close relationship with a competitor's member of staff.

For this to amount to SOSR, remember that there does need to be a genuine risk that the relationship will lead to the sharing of damaging confidential information. Usually, this comes down to the type of information the employee has access to and how close the connection is between the employee and the competitor. For example, a tribunal is unlikely to find dismissal fair if a junior employee has limited access to confidential information and only a distant connection to a competitor's employee.

Whether the tribunal considers the connection to be close will depend on the facts of each case. However, a husband-wife relationship is more likely to justify dismissal than a parent-child relationship (*Weal v Insulpak*) or that between next-door neighbours.

As usual, the fairness of the dismissal will very much depend on the context and the reasonableness of the employer's actions. For example, in *Simmons v*

SD Graphics Ltd, the EAT said that an employee who worked as a filing clerk and would see quotations, tenders and other confidential communications as part of her job was fairly dismissed for SOSR when her partner – a senior sales manager – moved to work for an aggressive competitor.

However, in *Skyrail Oceanic Ltd v Coleman*, the EAT held that the dismissal of a booking clerk by a travel agent because she married someone employed by a rival was unfair. Although the risk to the business was substantial (the employee had access to almost all of the employer's confidential information), the employee had provided an undertaking not to divulge confidential information and therefore the actual risk of disclosure was low.

Fair procedure

In terms of a fair procedure for conflict of interest, as well as the usual steps (see 'Personality clash', above), additional tips include the following:

- Focus your investigation on:
  - * How long the employee has had access to confidential information — and the type of information
  - * The nature of the relationship between the employee and the competitor

* The severity of the impact on the business if the information was disclosed

- Consider alternatives to dismissal, such as undertakings by the employee that they will not disclose the information or moving them to a position without access to confidential information.

- Only dismiss as a last resort.

Breakdown in trust and confidence

Sometimes, it is tempting to throw in the towel with an employee and dismiss them based on the feeling that the relationship is so damaged you no longer have any faith (or 'trust and confidence') in them.

This could be a fair SOSR. However, such a lack of clarity is not popular with courts or tribunals. It is seen as a bit lazy, as there will usually be a different (and more accurate) fair reason at the heart of the dismissal. It is more helpful to focus on the specific conduct or performance issue (which is what the underlying problem normally is) rather than to resort to the generality of 'loss of trust and confidence'.

For example, in *Leach v OFCOM*, the Court of Appeal criticised the employer for relying on the 'breakdown in trust and confidence' as the reason for dismissal. It said that, in fact, the real reason for dismissal was the employer's fear that if police disclosures about the employee's former involvement in child abuse became public, it would cause significant damage to its reputation.

That said, all is not lost for this SOSR reason. Despite the mislabelling in *Leach*, the dismissal was still found to be fair. Further, there are some (albeit rare) occasions where trust and confidence is the right label to attach.

In *Hutchinson v Calvert*, the EAT considered that the employer – a severely disabled man – was entitled to decide that his relationship with his carer had broken down to such an extent that it was irretrievable. This was particularly so given the need for such a close physical relationship. In this case, the breakdown was genuinely the reason for dismissal. There was no other reason for it: the employee was not, for example, guilty of misconduct nor had they behaved inappropriately. The relationship had just become frayed.

In *Huggins v Micrel Semiconductor (UK)*, the EAT upheld the tribunal's finding that the accumulation of a design engineer's unhelpful behaviour led to his fair dismissal. The employee, who had done little to help repair his poor relationship with the employer, refused to produce a medical report and instead sent an angry letter undermining the management of the company. The employer was entitled to consider this behaviour to be the final straw, which resulted in a breach of the implied term of mutual trust and confidence entitling it to dismiss.

If the reason for dismissal is genuinely a breakdown in trust and confidence, as usual, the decision to dismiss will still need to be reasonable, including following a fair procedure.

Fair procedure

As well as the usual steps, additional tips include the following:

- Try to repair the trust and confidence, for example, through consultation, mediation or training.

- Consider alternatives to dismissal, such as redeployment to another location or team, making changes to the employee's role or changing reporting lines.

Only if the relationship is irreparable and the situation cannot continue will a SOSR dismissal likely be fair.

CHAPTER 6

Fixed-term contracts

Ending a fixed-term contract seems pretty straightforward: the contract lasts for a defined length of time and then ends. However, as usual with employment law, it's not quite that easy.

The termination, expiry or non-renewal of these contracts counts as a dismissal under the *Employment Rights Act 1996*. This means that if you get the ending wrong – and the employee has two or more years' service – then they can bring an unfair dismissal claim. Also, bear in mind that a series of back-to-back fixed-term contracts for the same employer will count as one period of continuous employment.

To get the ending right, first, identify why you are not renewing the contract. That is, 'what is the real reason for dismissal?'.

For example, if you took the employee on to complete or perform a particular type of work that is no longer required – for example, fruit picking in the summer — the non-renewal of the contract will likely be by reason of redundancy. So, if the employee has two years' service, you will need to follow a fair redundancy procedure and pay a statutory redundancy payment.

However, if you want to terminate (or not renew) a fixed-term contract because you are dissatisfied with the employee's capability or conduct, then the right route to dismissal is by following the capability, performance improvement or disciplinary procedures.

Where there is no redundancy situation – so no reduction in roles or type of work – or a performance or misconduct issue, then SOSR will likely be your best bet. However, it is not a get-out-of-jail-free card. It only works if the fixed-term contract has a specific and genuine purpose, which is explained to the employee at the outset, and the contract ends when the purpose does.

In *Fay v North Yorkshire County Council*, the Court of Appeal held the employee's dismissal was fair for SOSR. She had been told the (genuine) purpose of her fixed-term contract at the outset (to cover a staff member's temporary absence) and the contract was terminated when the staff member returned to work.

However, in *West Midlands Regional Health Authority v Guirguis*, the EAT held that the dismissal of a locum consultant radiologist was unfair as the employer did not have a fair or genuine reason to dismiss. Although the employer said the regional health officer no longer wanted to employ locums (and therefore the purpose of the contract had ended), this was not true. In fact, locums were still being employed (and often for a longer period than the employee was engaged for).

Of course, as already explored, establishing SOSR as a potentially fair reason is only the start of the journey to a fair dismissal. Under section 98(4) of the *Employment Rights Act 1996*, the decision to dismiss for SOSR must also be reasonable in all the circumstances. This includes following a fair procedure.

Fair procedure

As already outlined, a fair SOSR procedure should generally include:

- Investigation
- Meeting(s) with the employee
- Warning(s) that dismissal is a possible outcome

- The right to appeal

More specifically, when dealing with the expiry of fixed-term contracts, employers should:

- Clarify in writing to the employee the purpose and expiry date of their fixed-term contract and any notice period which applies.

- Have a system in place to remind the employer in good time when the expiry date (or date to give notice) is approaching.

- Write to remind the employee that their contract is due to expire and the reasons for the proposed non-renewal.

- Consult with the employee, including inviting them to one or more meetings at which they can put forward suggestions to avoid expiry and non-renewal.

- Look for alternatives to dismissal and inform the employee of employment options within the company, including other temporary positions. This could also include helping the employee apply for a permanent post, particularly if this replaces their temporary fixed-term role.

Temporary replacements

Where a fixed-term contract is used to provide cover for temporary absence in the following circumstances, dismissing employees providing that cover may be automatically fair for SOSR (under section 106 of the *Employment Rights Act 1996*):

- Medical or maternity suspension
- Pregnancy or childbirth (maternity leave)
- Adoption leave
- Shared parental leave

To rely on this provision, the employer needs to inform the replacement employee in writing – at the time they are recruited – that their employment will terminate when the other employee returns to work. The reason for the replacement's dismissal needs to be to allow the original employee to return.

You probably won't need to use this often, though. The employee will still need the usual two years' service to claim unfair dismissal and there are not many employers who allow their staff to be off work that long for the above reasons.

Fair procedure

If you do use this provision, you will still need to follow a fair procedure. This is similar to the process outlined in 'Fixed term contracts', above. However, the focus will need to be on looking for alternative employment. There will be limited scope to avoid termination by any other means, given the need to make way for the returning employee.

CHAPTER 7

Mistakes or ignorance of the law

Although HR professionals are expected to get the law right most of the time, sometimes even the best can get things wrong! The good news is that all may not be lost: a dismissal based on a genuine mistake can be fair for SOSR. However, you will need a good reason for the mistake.

Right to work

The process of carrying out right-to-work checks and dismissals for illegal working provides fertile ground for mistakes (and for SOSR rescues), given how fiendishly complex immigration law can be. Trying to balance the duty of employers to prevent illegal working with the employee's right not to be unfairly dismissed is a minefield.

Where an employer is certain that an employee does not have, or has lost, their right to work, they can rely on 'illegality' as a fair reason for dismissal under section 98(2)(d) of the *Employment Rights Act 1996*. In these circumstances, the employee will not be able to continue in employment without breaking the law.

However, it is sometimes not entirely clear whether the employee does (or does not) have the right to work. This uncertainty means employers are often better off relying on SOSR as the fair reason for dismissal. Rather than needing to prove the employee did not have the right to work, the employer just has to show they had a 'genuine and reasonable belief' that this was the case. This allows employers to dismiss fairly for SOSR, even if it turns out the employee does have the right to work.

For example, in *Klusova v London Borough of Hounslow*, the employee was dismissed when her leave to remain in the UK expired. The Court of Appeal rejected the employer's justification of the dismissal based on 'illegality' as the employee did have the right to work as she had applied to extend her leave to remain. However, the court said that SOSR was a potentially fair reason for dismissal: the employee was dismissed due to a genuine but mistaken belief that it would have been illegal to continue to employ her.

Fair procedure

A fair procedure in the context of right-to-work issues is likely to include:

- Investigation – in this case into the employee's immigration and right-to-work status

- Meeting(s) with the employee to allow them to provide evidence of their right to work

- Warning(s) that dismissal is a possible outcome

- Carrying out relevant checks with the Home Office, such as via its Employers Checking Service

- The right to appeal

Other examples

Although an employee's right to work is the most common example of when SOSR is used in the context of mistakes, there are no limits on its use. Other examples include:

- **Dismissal of an employee where the employer had a genuine, if mistaken, belief that the employee was guilty of misconduct**. In *Farrant v Woodroffe School*, the employers insisted on a change of duties in breach of the employee's contract – they had been wrongly advised they had a legal right to do so. When the employee refused to work to the new job description, the employer dismissed them. The EAT decided that the dismissal was fair as the employer had made a genuine mistake based on wrong advice.

- **Mistaken understanding that an employee had resigned**. In *Ely v YKK Fasteners (UK) Ltd*, the Court of Appeal said it was fair for the employer to treat the employment as terminated when the employee said he would be resigning as he had been offered employment in Australia. He only told the employer he had changed his mind at a late stage after a replacement had already been engaged and trained.

CHAPTER 8

TUPE dismissals

In essence, the *Transfer of Undertakings (Protection of Employment) Regulations 2006* – better known as TUPE – protect the rights of employees when the whole or part of the business they work for transfers from their current employer ('transferor') to a new employer ('transferee').

If an employee is dismissed when the sole or principal reason is the transfer, this will be automatically unfair (for employees with two years' service), with no room for any SOSR defence or legal to-ing and fro-ing about whether it was reasonable.

To add to the complexity, you don't just need to take care with actual dismissals. The rules on automatic unfair dismissal also extend to constructive dismissals, where the employee resigns in response to a fundamental breach of contract that is a result of the transfer. In fact, there does not even have to be a breach of contract. It is enough that the transfer results in a 'substantial change to [the employee's] working conditions to their material detriment' under regulation 4(9) of TUPE.

The understandable upshot is that many employers try to avoid dismissal at the time of a TUPE transfer. This is not always commercially viable, but the good news is that all is not lost. Dismissals may be fair where the employer can show that they were carried out for an 'economic, technical or organisational (ETO) reason' which 'entails changes in the workforce'. In this case, the dismissal is potentially fair – either for SOSR or redundancy (depending on the circumstances) – as long as the employer can show it has acted reasonably.

This topic is covered in more detail in Book 5 of the Employment Law Library, 'Deconstructing TUPE'. There is also a free video guide that you can access on YouTube – search for 'Daniel Barnett Deconstructing TUPE'.

What is an ETO reason?

There is no statutory definition of 'economic, technical or organisational reason', but there is government guidance (www.gov.uk/government/publications/tupe-a-guide-to-the-2006-regulations). This suggests that to be an ETO reason, it must be for one of the following:

- **An economic reason:** Relating to the profitability or market performance of the new employer's business, for example, essential cost-saving requirements where profits have fallen to such a level that the business cannot continue trading without dismissing employees (most likely for redundancy).

- **A technical reason:** Relating to the nature of the equipment or production processes that the new employer uses, for example, where increased use of AI, computerisation or other mechanisation of tasks reduces the number of employees needed to carry out a particular function, or the transferring employees do not have the required skills.

- **An organisational reason:** Relating to the management or organisational structure of the new employer's business, for example, a business reorganisation or restructuring that results in redundancies, or dismissal in circumstances where it is impractical for employees to transfer to the new employer because of its location.

Importantly, an ETO reason must relate to a change in the day-to-day running of the business carrying out the dismissals and justify dismissals based only on its own reasons. For example, in

Wheeler v Patel, the EAT held that dismissals carried out by the current employer to satisfy the new employer's request to reduce the workforce (and get a higher price for the business) did not amount to an ETO reason. Since the ETO defence could not be established, the dismissals were therefore automatically unfair.

An ETO reason also needs to 'entail changes in the workforce' that are necessary and intentionally planned — not just a side effect. These can include a change in the location of the business or number of staff (i.e. redundancies) or otherwise a significant change in the functions performed by a number of the transferring employees.

For example, in *Nationwide Building Society v Benn and others*, the employees were financial planning and regional sales managers whose roles and responsibilities were downgraded post-transfer to fit within the new employer's structure. The employees resigned and claimed they had been constructively dismissed. The EAT held their dismissals were not unfair because the change in job functions was for an organisational reason that entailed changes in the workforce.

That said, if detrimental changes to contracts are made to ensure that all staff have the same terms and conditions of employment ('harmonisation'), this is unlikely to amount to an ETO.

Fair procedure

As usual, having a potentially fair reason for dismissal – in this case an ETO reason – is only half the battle. The dismissal still needs to be reasonable in all the circumstances, including following the right, fair procedure.

Often, TUPE dismissals will be for redundancy, as they will be due to a reduction in the number of roles or type of work available. In this case, remember to follow a redundancy procedure, including fair selection, consultation (individual and collective), looking for alternative employment and redundancy payments.

However, there are times when dismissals occur where the number of roles and work will remain stable. This is where SOSR comes into play. The steps to follow in a fair SOSR procedure will depend on the circumstances. For example, if you need to change the functions of the transferring staff, any subsequent dismissals (either constructive or actual) are likely to be the result of making contractual changes. This means the appropriate steps for a fair procedure will likely include:

- Meeting and consulting with affected staff
- Trying to secure their agreement to the changes

- Exploring alternatives to dismissal (including alternative employment)
- Offering to re-engage
- The right to appeal

CHAPTER 9

Other SOSR dismissals

Client or third-party pressure

External pressure, for example from a client or supplier, can amount to SOSR – but this will depend on a number of factors, including:

- Weighing up the client or other third party's business value – and the impact if it was lost – against the injustice to the employee were they dismissed.

- Showing that the employer was under serious pressure to dismiss and that this was genuinely coming from the client or other third party (rather than from the employer itself).

- The extent to which the employer tried to change the client or third party's mind.

- Whether there were any alternatives to dismissal, such as suspension or location change.

Whether the employer has the contractual right to remove the employee.

Fair procedure

For this type of dismissal to be fair, the employer will need to include:

- Consulting with the employee about the external pressure to dismiss and giving them the opportunity to put forward suggestions to avoid dismissal

- Exploring alternatives to dismissal with the employee, including a change to their role or location

- The right to appeal

Employee in prison

Having an employee in prison is not good news for anyone. Not only does an employer have all the usual problems associated with absence but also it is not good for morale or reputation.

It is therefore not surprising that many employers react by dismissing the imprisoned employee. However, it's important to understand there's no automatic right to do so. To fairly dismiss in these circumstances, the reason usually needs to relate to:

- The employee's conduct, where it has a sufficiently serious impact on their suitability to do their job and/or work relationships.

- A statutory duty or restriction prohibiting the employment from being continued, for example, where the employee works with children or young adults and the criminal offence means they are now barred from doing so.

- The inability of the employee to perform the contract of employment. This is known as 'frustration' of contract but is only applicable when the employee is likely to be in prison for a very long time. It is an automatic termination rather than a dismissal.

If it is unlikely that any of these apply, then SOSR is your next best bet.

The first point to consider is whether the employee's imprisonment puts the employer's reputation at risk. However – as explored in Chapter 5 – to justify dismissal, the risk posed to the employer's reputation needs to be really severe and have the potential to cause substantial harm to its business interests.

Otherwise, whether dismissal can be justified for SOSR depends on the circumstances surrounding the offence and how the employee's conviction and imprisonment impact their employment and the business as a whole.

For example, in *Kingston v British Railways Board*, an employee who had been sentenced to three months in prison for a violent assault on a police officer was found to have been fairly dismissed for SOSR. This was due to the serious nature of the offence causing a breakdown in trust and confidence between the employer and the employee, and the fact that imprisonment meant the employee would be unable to attend work (although for too short a period to be said to 'frustrate' the contract).

Also, in *Rangwani v Birmingham Heartlands and Solihull NHS Trust*, the employer was found to have fairly dismissed for SOSR an employee who was imprisoned for two months before being released on bail. The employee was a doctor who was charged with conspiring to murder his mistress – using drugs – and the employment tribunal said that the dismissal was fair. Patients would find it concerning to be treated by a doctor facing serious criminal charges involving the misuse of drugs.

Fair procedure

For the dismissal to be fair, the employer will need to follow the usual fair procedure, which is likely to include:

- Investigation into the reasons for the imprisonment, the nature of the offence and the length of sentence. This could include visiting the employee to hear their side of the story or at least asking them to provide their comments in writing.

- Meeting(s) with the employee (if possible, perhaps via video or phone calls) to present the findings of the investigation and allow them to have their say.

- Warning(s) of the risk of dismissal.

- Taking into account, for example, the:
  - * Impact the offence has on the employee's continued suitability for their role and relations with colleagues or clients.
  - * Employee's previous track record and length of service.
  - * Effect of the employee's absence on the business.

- Considering alternatives to dismissal (for example, a different role or location).

- The right to appeal.

CHAPTER 10

Summary

There is – as this book illustrates – no one-size-fits-all answer when considering whether SOSR is the right choice for a dismissal that is tricky to categorise.

These tips should help you decide, but if in any doubt seek legal advice.

- Carefully consider the *real* reason for dismissal – mislabelling can lead to errors in procedure.

- Follow the steps in the flow chart in Chapter 2 to help you decide.

- There's no limit to the type of scenario when SOSR could apply, but it does need to be sufficiently serious to justify dismissal.

- Try not to rely on a breakdown in trust and confidence as a stand-alone reason to dismiss.

- Whatever the reason for dismissal, always carry out a fair procedure first.

- Remember there is no off-the-peg fair SOSR procedure.

- If the reason fits within the common categories explored in this book, take into account the suggested steps for a fair procedure.

- If not, consider the general suggestions for a fair SOSR procedure.

- If any parts of the Acas Code may apply, include these in your fair procedure.

- Consider alternatives to dismissal.

- Remember that dismissal should generally be a last resort.

Also by
Daniel Barnett

Available on Amazon
or visit
go.danielbarnett.com/books

JOIN DANIEL EVERY SATURDAY EVENING AT
9PM WHEN HE PRESENTS THE

LBC Legal Hour
— OR CATCH UP VIA THE GLOBAL PLAYER,
AT bit.ly/lbclegalhour

SATURDAYS, 9PM

Dear HR Professional,

I take my hat off to you.

Having supported the HR community for so many years, I know It's a challenging job you do, sometimes under really difficult circumstances.

The tricky HR issues you have to handle must take up a tremendous amount of your time, your energy and your brain power. I bet it can be exhausting for you to work under that level of pressure.

Being An HR Professional In Today's Business Environment Is TOUGH!

Maintaining your high standards of professionalism must be a real struggle, especially when your efforts and expertise often go unappreciated.

I'll wager you have to make decisions on challenging HR situations you've sometimes never encountered before. Even if you're part of a team, it must sometimes feel like you're working in isolation.

With so much complexity and ambiguity, do you ever find you're not clear whether you're doing the right thing when there's so much to think about?

I expect it can be draining too. You've got to make tough decisions which may be unpopular.

The pressure's on you to ensure people are treated fairly while the business complies with its legal obligations.

It's a thankless task, especially if you've got grief coming at you from all sides.

Doubt can creep in too. Even though you're an extremely competent professional, you might even begin to question yourself...What if you've got it wrong?

You've got to cope with all that, whilst constantly having to convince any doubting stakeholders you're adding value to the business.

That pressure must take its toll on you.

You wouldn't be human if it didn't cause you tension, stress or even worse!

Being the caring professional you are, I bet you often take work home with you.

If You're Not Careful The Stress WILL Creep Up On You

And I don't just mean opening your laptop on your couch when everyone else is watching Eastenders.

We all know of families and relationships that come a poor second to the pressures and challenges faced at work.

Yours too..?

But does it have to be that way?

Should you feel the responsibility of the HR world is entirely on your shoulders and that you've got to bear that burden alone?

The answer is a firm no.

It doesn't have to be like that.

There Is An Answer To Help Make Your Work & Your Life Much Easier For You

There's a place you can get all the help, support, advice and encouragement you need to ease the constant pressure you have to bear.

IT'S CALLED THE HR INNER CIRCLE.

It will lift the burden you're carrying by giving you swift access to comprehensive resources and live practical guidance you can implement right away.

It's information I know will save you time, energy and effort.

It's a vibrant, active community of caring, like minded HR professionals willing to help you.

There are resources packed full of practical, actionable advice for you that's difficult to find anywhere else.

And it doesn't matter what you're working on.

Whether it be workforce engagement, attracting and keeping talent, diversity and inclusion or employee health and well being, you'll find support for all of that.

You're covered even if you're working on one of those tricky, sensitive, people problems you never see coming until they land squarely on your plate.

Timely Support To Make Your Job Easier, Can Be Rapidly Found In The HR Inner Circle

As a member of the HR Inner Circle, to get the support you want…

…just ask.

Your first port of call is the vibrant Facebook group, bursting at the seams with incredible HR professionals like you.

Just post your question and let it bubble and simmer in the collective genius of the group.

By the end of the day, you'll have at least 3-5 comments on your post, often more.

You'll get relevant, insightful and practical guidance that comes from the hard earned experience of your fellow members.

Often you'll get a response within a couple of hours. Sometimes you'll get an answer within minutes - even if it's late in the evening!

This highly active community never fails to astound me with just how willing they are to help fellow HR professionals like you.

They readily and generously share their hard earned knowledge and experience.

You Can Get Answers From Real People Quickly AND From Our Extensive Resource Library Too

...really important for someone working on their own who needs to check things out, or just bounce a few ideas around.

- Quentin Colborn
Director, QC People Management Ltd

While you wait for a response from the Facebook group, you'll likely find answers in the resource-rich members' vault on our secure online portal as well.

It takes just 2 clicks and a quick keyword search using our Rapid Results Search Tool.

You'll instantly find precisely where your topic is covered in our extensive back catalogue of monthly magazines and audio seminars.

In under 30 seconds you can find exactly what you're after.

It's that quick and easy.

...And if you need a specific legal insight?

Then pose your question live to an expert employment lawyer in our monthly Q&A session.

It'll either be me or one of my prominent contemporaries. You'll get your answer immediately without having to pay any legal costs.

If you can't wait, you'll find where it's been answered before with a quick search of previous Q&A sessions.

Our clever index system means you can find a question, and in a single click get straight to the recorded answer.

But perhaps you need to dive deep and explore the different options open to you to solve a particularly tricky problem?

Then join one of our monthly HR Huddles. There you can run your specific situation past other HR professionals.

They'll offer their insights, share their experience and work WITH you to find a solution that works FOR you.

You'll find all of this in one convenient place - the HR Inner Circle.

I've spent years practising law and have become recognised as one of the UK's leading employment law barristers. I've even got my own radio show!

It's Been A Labour Of Love Putting The HR Inner Circle Together So It Works For Professionals Like You

It's great to see that we all experience tricky cases from time to time.

- Annabelle Carey
Managing Consultant,
HR Services Partnership

But more importantly for you, I've also developed another skill.

It's bringing useful employment expertise AND practical experience together in a way that supports busy, overworked (and sometimes stressed) HR professionals like you.

Everything you're likely to need is **literally at your fingertips.**

This will save you time, energy and effort.

Being a member also means your business and clients will see you as even MORE INFORMED about the intricacies of employment law.

They'll marvel at how well you keep up to date when you're busy working so hard for them.

You'll be seen making quicker decisions and implementing effective solutions to accelerate the growth of the organisation.

You'll make impressive time and cost savings for the business.

And those tricky, off-piste situations you've never come across before..?

Well, nothing will faze you, because you're backed up by an HR support system second to none.

But more importantly, you'll feel that pressure gently ease off.

With the relief you'll feel knowing that such great help and guidance is just a few minutes, you'll wonder how you survived without it!

Here's what you get when you join the HR Inner Circle:

That's Why I'm Inviting You To Join And Reap The Many Rewards Of Membership

WWW.HRINNERCIRCLE.CO.UK

Benefit #1 - you'll get unlimited access to the hugely popular HR Inner Circle Facebook Private Group

* Tap into the vast wealth of knowledge, experience, insight and wisdom of the top 0.5% of your profession at any time, day or night.

* In less than 5 minutes you can post ANY HR question and get insightful answers and suggestions in a couple of hours or less, from some of the best in your profession.

* Fast track your impact by discovering effective shortcuts and workarounds from HR people who've been "there" and done "it".

* Expand and deepen your network of like minded individuals, secure in the knowledge they're as dedicated and as ambitious as you.

- Increase your prestige with your colleagues and stakeholders by being part of such an exclusive and prominent HR community.

- Gain confidence in your judgment and decisions by using the highly responsive community as a sounding board for your ideas.

Benefit #2 - you'll receive 11 copies of the HR Inner Circular Magazine every year

- Enjoy that satisfying "THUD" on your door mat every month when the postman delivers your very own copy of the HR Inner Circular magazine.

- Quickly discover exactly what the law says about key issues affecting HR professionals around the UK like you.

- Get concise and practical guidance on how employment law applies to the challenging situations and circumstances you deal with every day.

- Avoid the mistakes of others by applying the lessons from the in depth analysis of real life case studies.

- Benefit from a legal deep dive by the UK's leading employment law barrister into a topical employment question posed by a fellow member (perhaps you!).

- Review a summary of recent important Facebook Group discussions worthy of sharing, that you may have missed.

- Explore a range of related and relevant topics useful for your practice and your broader professional development.

The magazine is really informative, the Facebook group such a community, and I think exceptional value for money.

- Lis Moore
Head of Advisory & Support Services,
Society of Local Council Clerks

Benefit #3 - Monthly Audio Seminars

- A 60 minute legal deep dive by me into an important subject relevant to you and your practice.

- Professionally recorded content recorded exclusively for the HR Inner Circle - you'll not find this information anywhere else.

- Carefully structured content that's easy to consume, understand and apply in your work as an HR professional.

- Episodes delivered every month so you can stay current on the latest issues affecting HR professionals.

- The convenience of listening to the recording online or downloading the mp3 for later enjoyment at a time suitable to your busy schedule (perfect for any commute).

Benefit #4 - you get an exclusive invite to a live online Q&A Session every fortnight, led by an expert employment lawyer

- Gain 60 minutes of live and direct access to the sharpest legal minds from my secret little black book of contacts.

- Get answers to your knottiest employment law questions, and solutions to your trickiest HR problems, from some of the brightest employment lawyers in the UK.

- Avoid having to pay the £300-£400 it would cost you to ask a lawyer your question outside of the HR Inner Circle.

- Benefit from valuable insights from the answers given to other members.

- If you can't attend live, watch the recording when it's convenient for you.

- Quickly access the recorded answer to any question asked in the session by simply clicking the question index for that session.

- Save time by downloading the session transcription to scan-read at a time suitable for you.

Benefit #5 - join a live Monthly Huddle with other HR Professionals to solve your most challenging HR problems

- Attend your very own mini-mastermind group of highly qualified, highly regarded and experienced fellow HR professionals to "group think" through an issue you're facing right now.

- Develop bespoke solutions to the unique problems and challenges you have to deal with in a safe, supportive and confidential environment.

- Feel safe knowing these online zoom calls are NOT recorded to respect the sensitivity of issues addressed and the privacy of those involved. [NOTE - a professional transcriber attends and takes written notes. An anonymised summary is then made available to the membership]

- Recent Huddle topics included changing employee benefits, mandatory vaccination, career breaks, sickness during disciplinaries, effective worker forums and hybrid working arrangements.

Benefit #6 - access our Templates & Resources Centre

- Gain immediate access to our library of the most popular and frequently used forms, assessments, agreements, checklists, letter templates, questionnaires and reports to help the busiest HR professionals save time and get things done quicker and easier.

- Download them as Word documents, so you can edit and personalise them to fit your business needs

- New templates added every single month

Benefit #7 - build your own Employment Law Library

- We send you several brand-new books on employment law several times each year

- Acquire your own physical library of concise, easy-to-read and fully updated textbooks

- Recent titles include Hiring Staff, Managing Sickness Absence, Spotting Malingering and Resolving Grievances

Benefit #8 - free Ticket to our Annual Conference

- The perfect opportunity to extend your personal network of fellow HR professionals.

- Meet up face to face with the people who've been supporting you in the Facebook Group and HR Huddles so you can deepen those connections even further.

- Gather key insights and takeaways to help you personally and professionally from some of the best speakers on the circuit. Previous speakers have covered motivation, dealing with difficult people, goal setting and productivity, decision making and social media marketing.

- Get instant access to recordings of all previous conferences so even if you can't attend in person, you can benefit from the event in your own time.

- Includes probably the best conference lunch you'll ever have - a bold claim I know, but we use outstanding caterers.

It never ceases to amaze me the amount
of time and effort people put into the
Facebook group, sharing their experiences,
advice, and sage words of wisdom.

- Emma Lister
HR Consultant, SME HR Services

Benefit #9 - your Personal Concierge will help you get the best out of your membership

- You get personal access to Nina who'll point you in the direction of exactly where to find what you need. She's supported hundreds of members over the 5 years she's been part of the team.

- Nina also works closely with the 11 back office staff that support the operation. In the extremely unlikely event she doesn't know where something is, she knows who will.

HOW MUCH DOES JOINING THE HR INNER CIRCLE COST?

There's no doubt in my mind the annual value of membership benefits is in the many thousands of pounds range.

But you're not going to pay anywhere near that. Let me remind you of what that small monthly fee gives you every year

Access to the private Facebook Group	INCLUDED
HR Inner Circular Magazine subscription	INCLUDED
Monthly Audio Seminars	INCLUDED
Live Q&A sessions	INCLUDED
Monthly HR Huddles	INCLUDED
Templates & Resources Centre	INCLUDED
Employment Law Library	INCLUDED
Free ticket to the HR Inner Circle Annual Conference	INCLUDED
Your Personal Membership Concierge	INCLUDED

TOTAL   PRICELESS

Another way of looking at your investment is this:

Because access to what you need is so quick…

Join today and that price is fixed for as long as you remain a member. You'll always pay the same, even if we increase the price to new members (which we regularly do).

…it's like having your very own part time, legally trained, assistant HR Business Partner, just waiting to provide you with all the answers you need…

WWW.HRINNERCIRCLE.CO.UK

Plus, With Membership Of The HR Inner Circle, You'll Also Get These 4 Additional Resources For FREE!

Additional Resource #1 - Handling Awkward Conversations

A video case study masterclass you can share with managers to train them to handle awkward staff disciplinary, performance and attitude problems. A huge time saver for you.

Additional Resource #2 - 6 x HR Employment Online Courses

Immediate, on demand access to six thorough, online HR courses (with more constantly added), including Employment Tribunal Compensation, Chat GPT for HR Professionals, Deconstructing TUPE, Changing Terms & Conditions, Unconscious Bias At Work and Handling Grievances.

Additional Resource #3 - Free listing on the Register of Investigators

Advertise your professional investigations service in our member's portal.

Additional Resource #4 - Significant discounts on sets of policies, contracts, and other courses.

Get member discounts on my Getting Redundancy Right and HR Policies products as well as other price reductions as new products are released.

It's a really good investment. The support you get from other Facebook group members is fantastic. Whatever your question, someone will know the answer. Access to Daniel's experience and knowledge through the podcasts and Q&A is invaluable too.

- **Tracy Madgwick**
HR Consultant, Crafnant HR

I'm So Confident Joining The HR Inner Circle Is The Right Decision For You, Here's My

NO LIMITS

GUARANTEE

Take action and join the HR Inner Circle **now**.

If you're not 100% satisfied with your investment, you can cancel at ANY time.

Just tell us, and your membership will end immediately. No long-term contracts. No notice periods. No fuss.

I'm comfortable doing this because I know once you join, you'll find the support, the information and the strategies so useful, you'll never want to leave.

Before you decide though, let me be very clear about membership of the HR Inner Circle.

It's only for ambitious and dedicated HR professionals who want to accelerate and increase their impact by plugging into an HR ecosystem with its finger firmly on the pulse of what's working right now in HR.

If you're just plodding along and are content with just getting by, then this is probably not for you.

But if you're drawn to benefiting from standing shoulder to shoulder with some of the giants in the HR community who will help you solve your toughest problems, then joining the HR Inner Circle is the RIGHT decision for you.

Join here now:

WWW.HRINNERCIRCLE.CO.UK

Daniel Barnett

P.S. Remember when you join you get unrestricted access to the private Facebook group, the monthly magazine delivered direct to your door, the monthly audio seminar, regular free books, templates, checklists and resources, on-demand video courses, over 100 audio seminars and back copies of magazines, live interactive Q&A sessions with a lawyer, focused monthly huddles with other HR professionals, a free ticket to the annual conference, your personal concierge plus a bunch of additional resources...

Printed in Great Britain
by Amazon

44798163R00066